D1304204

DATE DUE

PRINTED IN U.S.A.

MY SENSES

Smell

LET'S READ
AV2
BY WEIGL
ADDED VALUE · AUDIO VISUAL

www.av2books.com

LET'S READ
AV²
BY WEIGL™
ADDED VALUE • AUDIO VISUAL

Go to **www.av2books.com**, and enter this book's unique code.

BOOK CODE

J763487

AV² by Weigl brings you media enhanced books that support active learning.

AV² provides enriched content that supplements and complements this book. Weigl's AV² books strive to create inspired learning and engage young minds in a total learning experience.

Your AV² Media Enhanced books come alive with...

Audio
Listen to sections of the book read aloud.

Video
Watch informative video clips.

Embedded Weblinks
Gain additional information for research.

Try This!
Complete activities and hands-on experiments.

Key Words
Study vocabulary, and complete a matching word activity.

Quizzes
Test your knowledge.

Slide Show
View images and captions, and prepare a presentation.

... and much, much more!

Published by AV² by Weigl
350 5th Avenue, 59th Floor, New York, NY 10118
Website: www.av2books.com   www.weigl.com

Library of Congress Cataloging-in-Publication Data

Durrie, Karen.
Smell / Karen Durrie.
p. cm. – (My senses)

ISBN 978-1-61913-311-2 (hard cover : alk. paper)
ISBN 978-1-61913-316-7 (soft cover : alk. paper)

1. Smell—Juvenile literature. I. Title.
QP458.D87 2013
612.8'6—dc23

                        2012000470

Printed in the United States of America in North Mankato, Minnesota
2 3 4 5 6 7 8 9 0   17 16 15 14 13

012013
WEP280113

Project Coordinator: Aaron Carr   Design: Mandy Christiansen

Weigl acknowledges Getty Images, iStock, and Dreamstime as image suppliers for this title.

Smell

In this book,
you will learn

- what smell is

- types of smell

- what smell tells you

and much more!

3

Smell is one of your five senses.
Senses help you learn
about the world around you.

4

You smell with your nose.

5

Smell tells you which smells you like.

A pine tree smells good.

A bakery smells good.

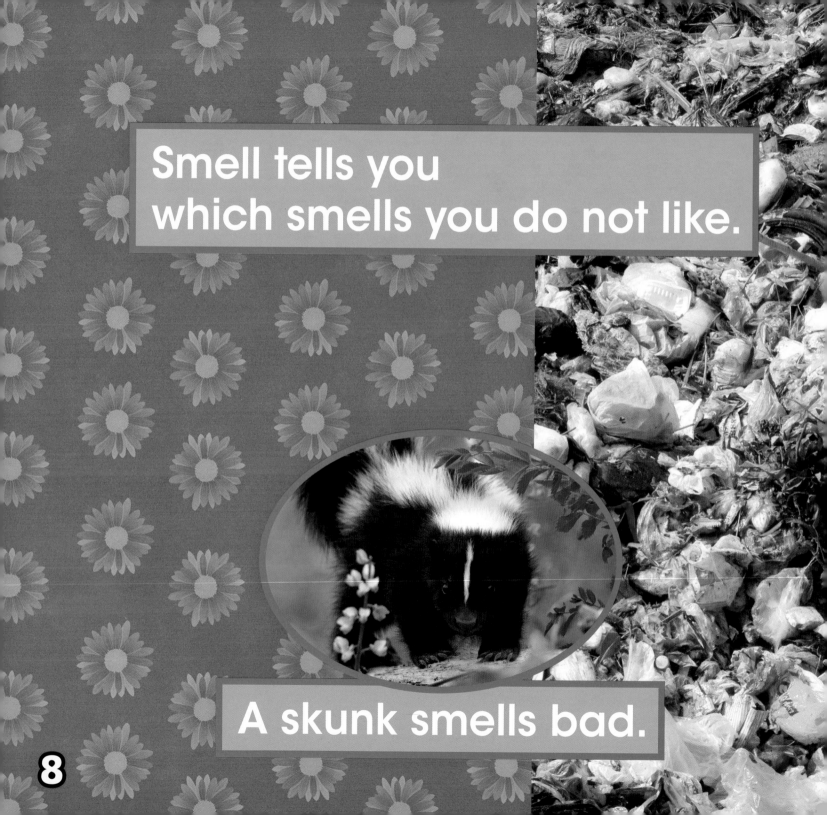

Smell tells you
which smells you do not like.

A skunk smells bad.

Garbage smells bad.

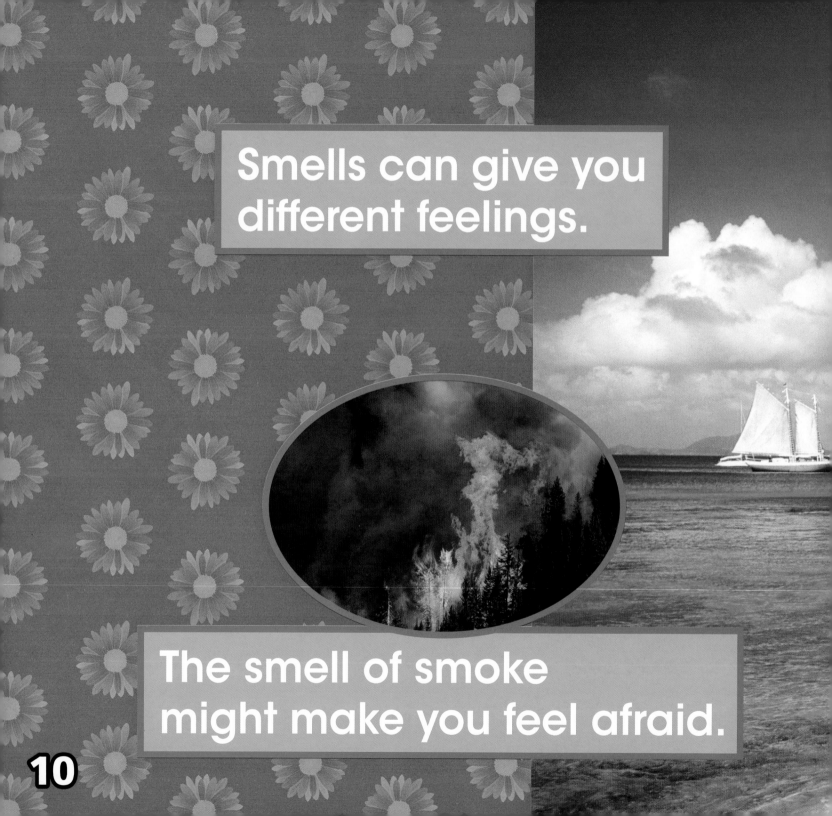

Smells can give you different feelings.

The smell of smoke might make you feel afraid.

The smell of the ocean
might make you feel happy.

Smells can change
how you feel.

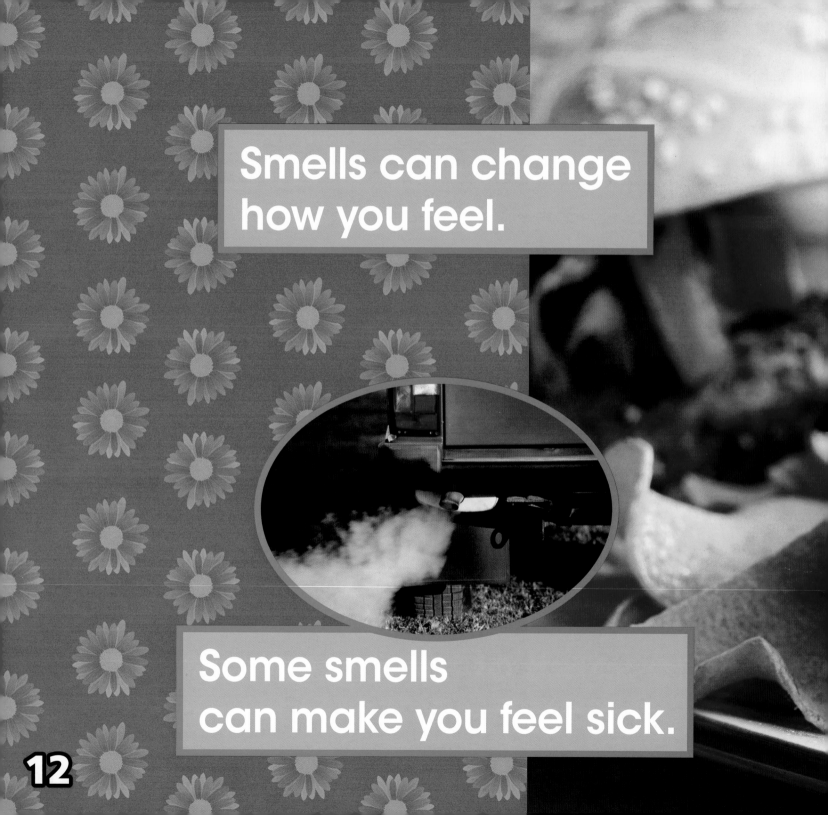

Some smells
can make you feel sick.

Some smells
can make you feel hungry.

13

Smells can make you remember times and places.

You may smell cake and think of a party.

You may smell flowers and think of summer.

The sense of smell is different for each person.

Your friend may not like the smell of a dog.

You may like the smell of a dog.

Smell can help you taste your food.

Lemons have a sour smell.

Candy has a sweet smell.

19

What smells might you find here?

Which things smell good?
Which things smell bad?

22

23

KEY WORDS

Research has shown that as much as 65 percent of all written material published in English is made up of 300 words. These 300 words cannot be taught using pictures or learned by sounding them out. They must be recognized by sight. This book contains 42 common sight words to help young readers improve their reading fluency and comprehension. This book also teaches young readers several important content words, such as proper nouns. These words are paired with pictures to aid in learning and improve understanding.

Sight Words

a	give	might	what
about	good	not	which
and	has	of	with
around	have	one	world
can	help	places	you
change	here	some	your
different	how	tells	
do	is	the	
each	learn	things	
find	like	think	
food	make	times	
for	may	tree	

Content Words

bakery	ocean
cake	party
candy	person
dog	senses
feelings	skunk
flowers	smell
friend	smoke
garbage	summer
lemons	
nose	

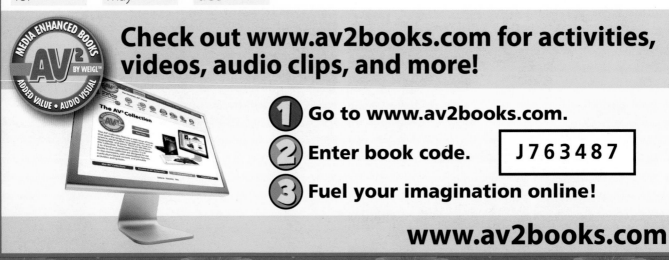

Check out www.av2books.com for activities, videos, audio clips, and more!

1 Go to www.av2books.com.

2 Enter book code. | J 7 6 3 4 8 7 |

3 Fuel your imagination online!

www.av2books.com